SHAFTED!

by John Godber

SAMUEL FRENCH

MUSIC USE NOTE

Licensees are solely responsible for obtaining formal written permission from copyright owners to use copyrighted music in the performance of this play and are strongly cautioned to do so. If no such permission is obtained by the licensee, then the licensee must use only original music that the licensee owns and controls. Licensees are solely responsible and liable for all music clearances and shall indemnify the copyright owners of the play(s) and their licensing agent, Concord Theatricals, against any costs, expenses, losses and liabilities arising from the use of music by licensees. Please contact the appropriate music licensing authority in your territory for the rights to any incidental music.

USE OF COPYRIGHT MUSIC

A licence issued by Concord Theatricals to perform this play does not include permission to use the incidental music specified in this copy. Where the place of performance is already licensed by the PERFORMING RIGHT SOCIETY (PRS) a return of the music used must be made to them. If the place of performance is not so licensed then application should be made to the PRS, 2 Pancras Square, London, N1C 4AG (www.prsformusic.com). A separate and additional licence from PHONOGRAPHIC PERFORMANCE LTD, 1 Upper James Street, London W1F 9DE (www.ppluk.com) is needed whenever commercial recordings are used.

IMPORTANT BILLING AND CREDIT REQUIREMENTS

If you have obtained performance rights to this title, please refer to your licensing agreement for important billing and credit requirements.

AUTHOR'S NOTE

There is clearly no doubt in most minds, that the Miners' Strike of 1984 had a seismic effect on the coalfields of the United Kingdom, and of West Yorkshire in particular. It was also responsible for an explosion of artistic expression which attempted, in a sense, to battle against the agony of such large scale industrial destruction, and to keep the cause alive in the minds of the public for as long as possible.

Though I was born into a mining family, with both my grandfathers and father being miners ironically, for me, the strike erupted at a time when I had left my mining background, to run a theatre company in Hull, a city which had already faced the Cod Wars, and consequently dwindling fishing grounds, which had in turn, lead to the demise of its once enormous fishing industry.

Though it was always on my radar I had, for many years, resisted from writing about the strike, since it was still very raw, and had driven a wedge through my own close knit family. Quite recently, however, I began to wonder where the artists and commentators, who had so vehemently voiced their feelings about the strike, had put down their pens, when it came to accounting for events which had happened in the twenty- five years since the strike. When the television cameras and journalists had long gone, and the people there were left to get on with their lives, where were the artists to paint the truth of Mrs. Thatcher's legacy?

Surprisingly little seems to have been published regarding the lives of the people who were left to deal with the aftermath, compared with what was produced about the 1984 strike. On a personal level, I had seen my father and mother, sister, aunty and uncle all try to rebuild their lives and their relationships after the heat of such a huge political struggle, and in more recent times, a kind of normality had returned to those mining villages which had been decimated, though wherever you looked, the effects of the strike were always apparent, though sometimes unspoken.

Shafted!, by no means a unbiased view of the legacy of the strike, is an attempt to rebalance the huge lack of documentation of what happened in the twenty-five years after the event, and give voice to the story of one partnership which was left to pick up the pieces after the savage closure of the pits. Dot and Harry are jobless at the top of Act I and have to try to make sense of the world ahead of them.

The play is told in a series of vignettes which progress from 1984 to 2014, with Act II travelling back in time to meet Act I at the interval. This retrospective structure serves to add a sense of aching irony to the play, which demonstrates how the mining communities, even without the actual presence of a mine, still has a magnetic pull on the people who once lived there, and give testament not only to their resilience, but to their dry ironic sense of humour.

John Godber OBE
Hull, 2018

SHAFTED!

First production was at Theatre Royal Wakefield Feb 2016. It was directed by John Godber and Neil Sissons with design by Grahame Kirk. The cast was as follows:

HARRY	John Godber
DOT	Jane Thornton

Subsequently the play went on a national tour.

Dedicated to my Dad, Harry Godber

CHARACTERS

DOT is a very effusive and optimistic miner's wife, who, as she ages loses her optimism and becomes sarcastic and bitter.

HARRY is a dour and ideologically immovable miner, who as he ages, becomes more sensitive and emotional.

SETTING

The action takes place in Upton and Bridlington.

TIME

In the years between 1984 and 2014.

ACT I

Scene One

Essentially an empty space, the back wall of the theatre is laid bare. Along the back wall are the props for the play which will be collected when appropriate and two dining chairs which are almost offstage. Some costume changes will be in full view, others off stage. Centre stage an open area which will translocate from 1984 to 2014. In the centre of this space is a green garden gate circa council houses from the late 1980s. This remains constant throughout Act I. Downstage left and right are white Yorkshire roses, these are set in wood on a black floor, and are referred to throughout the play. Upstage left and right of the central area are two flats on the stage right one an area which can be used to project captions, across from it, creating a shaft, is another flat which may have the feel of a council house estate about it.

There is no play over music.

House lights fade to blacks.

Haze fills the stage.

HARRY, *a miner in his forties, wearing track suit bottoms and a vest enters and takes a position left of the gate.* **DOT**, *his wife a woman in her forties, wearing appropriately inexpensive clothes takes position right of the gate.*

Caption.

UPTON. 1984.

Slowly the two of them speak. They are both lit by solitary overhead spotlights which gives them a ghostly feel.

BOTH The miners, united, will never be defeated!

The miners, united, will never be defeated,

The miners, united, will never be defeated!

There is a sadness in the delivery of this final line. As the lights fade very loud and aggressive music plays. **DOT** *exits.*

Music swells.*

Lights fade.

Black out.

---

* A licence to produce *Shafted!* does not include a performance licence for any third-party or copyrighted recordings. Licensees should create their own.

Scene Two

HARRY *stands at the gate to his house. He is terribly upset by the effects of the strike. He has stood at the garden gate for the last ten months, not knowing where to go or what to do. We see that he is a physical specimen hewn from hard work at the pit. He stands and looks out towards the rest of the estate he has lived on all his life.*

Caption.

UPTON 1985.

As the music fades up to a crescendo, **HARRY** *looks around the estate.*

Music swells.*

Lights fade.

Black out.

---

* A licence to produce *Shafted!* does not include a performance licence for any third-party or copyrighted recordings. Licensees should create their own.

Scene Three

HARRY *is still stood at the garden gate. Time however, has moved on and so has his mood, he is now in floods of tears, inconsolable. As he cries...*

Caption.

Upton. Two months later.

Lights fade.

Music swells.*

Black out.

____

* A licence to produce *Shafted!* does not include a performance licence for any third-party or copyrighted recordings. Licensees should create their own.

Scene Four

HARRY is still stood at the garden gate. He is lost but stoical, as he stands the music fades under. As the music fades we see: –

Caption.

Upton. Two months later.

As the music fades and the lights come up we see DOT enter, she is dressed in cheap clothes of the period. She is aggravated and brutally short with HARRY.

DOT You doing out here?

HARRY Nowt?

A beat.

DOT You alrate?

HARRY Yeh!

A beat.

DOT There's a fry up!

HARRY That's good then!

DOT Our Darren's rang, they're going up to t' caravan!

HARRY That's good then!

A beat.

DOT I've teld him it's leaking!

A beat.

HARRY We should get shut on it, throw it on t' tip like everything else round here!

DOT Oh we're off!

HARRY Forty-six and dumped?

DOT Aye, and nowt to show for it!

A beat.

It's cheese and egg!

A beat.

HARRY Cheese 'n egg?

A beat.

DOT Well I daren't go back down to Dennis Knowles', I owe him a hundred and fourteen quid on meat we've had during t' strike!

A beat.

Her next door's been down to t' soup kitchens, she sez we can still go down if we want!

HARRY Oh ar?

DOT A bloody year and we've still got soup kitchens!

HARRY When are they going to come and put that on't tele?

A beat.

DOT A bloody year!

HARRY And we're still waiting for a pay out!

DOT It said some had got thousands on't tele!

HARRY It sez all sorts!

A beat.

DOT Him next door's got next to nowt, she sez!

A beat.

HARRY I'll get about eighteen!

DOT Better than a kick up arse!

HARRY For thirty years?

A beat.

DOT Do you want some tomatoes with this then or what?

A beat.

HARRY Jeff Swifts got a job on t' council so they seh!

DOT Well go down and have a look that then!

HARRY Tha what?

A beat.

I wouldn't be seen dead working for t' council!

DOT *goes into the house.*

DOT What you gunna do then stand at garden gate for t' rest of your life?

HARRY I'll tell you what I'm going do...never work for t' bloody council!

DOT I'll throw this tea on t' fire back then shall I?

She has gone. **HARRY** *follows her.*

HARRY Hang on, I'm coming for it!

Music plays.*

Lights fade.

Black out.

---

* A licence to produce *Shafted!* does not include a performance licence for any third-party or copyrighted recordings. Licensees should create their own.

Scene Five

Lights come up to reveal **DOT** *sweeping the path with a yard brush. As she does* **HARRY** *with a change of top enters. He is carrying two steel dustbins.*

Caption.

UPTON. 1987.

DOT You've spilt half the sodding ash!

HARRY Give up you silly sod!

DOT You're the worse bin man in Wakefield Met!

HARRY Give up woman!

DOT Tracey's pregnant did our Darren seh?

HARRY Again?

DOT They must have nowt better to do!

HARRY They've nearly a football team naa...

DOT And t' fridge is broke!

HARRY Stick t' milk in grate then!

DOT That'd look good!

HARRY They're on about bringing wheelie bins in!

DOT We'll be posh then!

HARRY Ah we will, you'll have to wheel 'em art yussen! So work that out!

DOT I thought you were on t' Havercroft run, what you doing on Upton?

HARRY There's men short. Apparently Kenny Barrett hung hissen last neet, so Karl's had to move me. I hate being on t' Upton everybody can see what I'm doing!

DOT What's it matter, you're working!

HARRY When I wa' at pit nobody could see what I wa' doing!

DOT Why, what wa' you doing?

HARRY What did you think I was doing?

DOT At least you've got a job, him next door's still looking.

HARRY He's jumped out of the bedroom window twice hasn't he?

DOT Is he trying to kill hissen?

HARRY Either that to fly off!

A beat.

DOT What time are you back?

HARRY Late today, so we can be early on Friday.

A beat.

DOT My Mam sez we should go away!

HARRY Let's try and fly off wi' him next door then!

A beat.

DOT She sez we need a brek!

HARRY She gunna treat us?

DOT Not unless she leaves us sommat!

HARRY Well I don't want her false teeth.

DOT Neither does she, she never wears 'em!

A beat.

Have you seen the bloody mess you've made here?

HARRY *turns with the bins about to exit.*

I'm going to have to report you!

HARRY Don't be doing owt like that, they're looking to get rid o
men anyway, they don't need any encouragement!

DOT There's ash all over!

> **HARRY** *makes his way off stage slowly struggling with the bins.* **DOT** *sweeps as...*

HARRY What you put in here?

DOT Them weights out of our Darren's bedroom!

HARRY Aren't we bloody blessed with you, you're trying to bloody kill me and all!

> *Music swells*.*

> *Lights fade.*

> *Black out.*

---

* A licence to produce *Shafted!* does not include a performance licence for any third-party or copyrighted recordings. Licensees should create their own.

Scene Six

DOT *enters carrying a bucket and a sponge, she also has a shammy leather with her, she opens the gate and stands on the downstage edge of the gate.* HARRY *enters wearing a different vest top and carrying a large ladder.*

Caption.

WAKEFIELD. 1990.

HARRY *stands upstage of the gate with the ladder.*

DOT What about the back?

HARRY Sod the back!

DOT We can't just do half a job.

HARRY I'm not going around the back, there's dog shit all over!

DOT You're not scared of that are you?

HARRY It's the donkey tied to the dustbin that I'm worried about, not the dog shit, mind you have you seen the size of it?

A beat.

I bet the dog's bigger than the bloody donkey!

A beat.

DOT What are they doing with the donkey then?

HARRY Well I hope that they don't want the binmen to take it! They won't take cardboard anymore so they're snookered if they want that donkey to go!

DOT Who ties a donkey to a dustbin?

HARRY These silly sods!

A beat.

DOT How much have we got then?

HARRY *checks his pockets for cash.*

HARRY About thirty-seven quid!

DOT Most of these have been done, somebody's beaten us to best estates!

HARRY Well it was your idea to come out to Pinderfields! I said we should have gone out Sandal way, nobody knows us out there either!

DOT My Mam said she saw this estate when she went t' hospital.

HARRY There's a plague of bloody window cleaners round here and I worked with half o 'em, the silly sods can't think of owt else to do!

DOT Like us?

HARRY Exactly!

A beat.

DOT So how am I gunna get back then? Shall I get a taxi?

HARRY An' how much is that gunna cost?

A beat.

DOT I'll have to get t' bus then will I?

HARRY A taxi and all the money's gone hasn't it?

A beat.

DOT Why what are you going to do with the car?

HARRY Wait for our Darren to come and give me a push.

DOT What do you think's up with it?

HARRY Might be t' cylinder head, I don't know, but I said we should have never come out here!

DOT We need a new un!

HARRY Well we're not going to get one with thirty-seven quid are we?

DOT To be honest don't like being in with our Darren he never puts two hands on't wheel!

HARRY That bloody car he's got naa you're lucky it's got a bloody wheel!

DOT *rubs her hands.*

DOT Ruining my hands this!

HARRY Aye and mine.

DOT *laughs.*

DOT I better go and get bus then!

HARRY Better go and get bus then!

A beat.

DOT I'll look a right ha' peth on t' bus with a bucket and a shammy leather.

HARRY Well if you get a minute you could clean the windows, make some more cash while you're waiting!

DOT *starts to exit.*

DOT You think you're funny!

HARRY I wasn't being funny?

HARRY *remains.*

Music plays.*

Lights fade.

Black out.

---

* A licence to produce *Shafted!* does not include a performance licence for any third-party or copyrighted recordings. Licensees should create their own.

Scene Seven

In the black out **HARRY** *has made the ladder into a step ladder and is sat on it, he appears to be rolling a joint. As the lights come up* **DOT** *enters wearing a different top, she wears marigold gloves and carries a bucket, she wears a peaked cap.*

Caption.

WAKEFIELD. 1991.

DOT You doing?

HARRY Nowt

DOT Smoking?

HARRY It's only a little un!

DOT A little what?

HARRY A kid from darn Elmsall, Chris Cooper got me some, it's all rate!

DOT What is it?

HARRY It's only a bit of grass!

A beat.

DOT What sort o grass?

HARRY Grass, grass!

DOT Dope?

HARRY Alrate keep you voice darn!

DOT What you smoking dope for?

A beat.

HARRY I'm only having a whiff, it just takes t' edge off!

DOT 'Edge off what?

HARRY Cleaning windows for a start!

DOT Aren't we...

HARRY Walking t' streets!

DOT This is...

HARRY Carrying my ladder!

DOT Jeee...

HARRY Feeling like a knob head!

> *A beat.*

> Anyway, it's not illegal!

DOT It is!

HARRY Well aye it is; but I'm not hurting owt am I?

> *A beat.*

DOT How long you been smoking that shit?

HARRY I only have one a day!

DOT One a day?

HARRY Usually!

DOT Usually?

HARRY Hey, calm darn!

DOT Calm darn? You're sat here stoned and I'm slogging my guts out? I've done all these big bungalows, and you're just sat here!

HARRY You can have a go if you want!

DOT Bloody hell what's happening here?

HARRY Calm darn for Christ – sake tha'll have a frigging stroke!

DOT Tha'll be havin' a frigging stroke in a minute, I'll chuck this water all over you!

> **HARRY** *starts to chuckle.*

> What's up naa?

HARRY You?

DOT What?

HARRY You wi' that bucket, shouting at me!

DOT How many of them have you had?

HARRY I had one before I got up!

DOT Do you know, I thought I could smell sommat!

HARRY Then I had one when you went to put some flowers on your Pauline!

DOT At cemetery?

HARRY Hey in China miners were on heroin, so this is nowt, they never came up, there were opium dens darn t' pit! And they were happy wi' that, wa' t' authorities, as long as they were getting t' coal out! They just left 'em darn there, no idea what the frigging hell they were doing as long as they were getting t' coal out, they didn't give a toss! It's same on this job, who's bothered?

DOT This int rate though sat in't street!

HARRY I'll tell thee what's not rate, losing your livelihood through no fault of your own, that's what's not rate, so don't start telling me what's rate and what's not rate, coz tha doesn't know blob!

DOT I know I was there, I know I was on 'picket. I know I was going without just as much as anybody else and I know I'm not sat with my mind being addled smoking shit!

HARRY Hey it's not bad shit this. Chris told me it'd been seasoned with horse tranquilliser. So I sez I'll trot over to their house and try it!

> **HARRY** *breaks out into laughter.*

I'll trot over and try it I sez!

DOT I heard you!

HARRY You?

DOT What?

> **DOT** *turns away and is about to exit!*

HARRY Marry me!

> *A beat.*

DOT You're bloody crackers!

HARRY You right there!

> **HARRY** *laughs on the ladder.*

DOT Aren't we alrate wi' this?

HARRY Funny!

DOT No, it's not funny, if you want to know the truth: funny is not what it is, if you want to know the bloody truth, pathetic is what it is!

> **DOT** *storms off stage, as* **HARRY** *pulls a face at her.*
>
> *Music swells*.*
>
> *Light fade.*
>
> *Black out.*

---

* A licence to produce *Shafted!* does not include a performance licence for any third-party or copyrighted recordings. Licensees should create their own.

Scene Eight

HARRY *enters without his ladder, he stands at the gate, he is wearing a different vest. As he looks around at the gate* DOT *comes to him from the other side of the gate carrying a number of bags from the supermarket.*

Caption.

UPTON. 1992.

DOT Just been down to see if mi Mam's alrate, and pop into t' market before we get off!

A beat.

I'll dump this lot and we can get down' Ackworth, do Station Road, all big houses down there, can't move for money!

HARRY You'll have a job!

DOT Why, what's up?

A beat.

HARRY I've got shut!

DOT Eh?

HARRY I've let it go!

DOT What?

HARRY Ladder!

A beat.

DOT What for?

HARRY I thought you said you'd had enough?

DOT Well aye but...

HARRY Well then?

DOT What you done that for?

HARRY Couldn't stand it anymore!

A beat.

DOT Who you let it go to?

HARRY Him next door?

A beat.

DOT How much for?

HARRY For next to nowt!

DOT Next to nowt?

HARRY I've just let him give me twenty quid for it!

A beat.

DOT It was giving us a hundred quid a week, cash in hand!

A beat.

HARRY Well I've just let him have it!

DOT Are you sure you've not smoked it?

HARRY I've done him a good turn, he sez!

DOT Well go get it back!

HARRY I don't want to!

DOT Well what do you want to do?

A beat.

HARRY Nowt really!

DOT Jesus!

A beat.

HARRY Go back to t' pit!

DOT *becomes sympathetic.*

DOT Bloody hell!

A beat.

HARRY Chris sez there's some jobs up at Langthwaite counting bananas, I might go up there.

DOT Are you joking?

HARRY That's what him and Keith Johnson's doing he sez!

A beat.

DOT You want a job counting bananas?

HARRY I think there's pineapples and all, and apples, I don't think it's just bananas!

A beat.

DOT Have you been smoking?

HARRY I've only had one!

DOT Jeee...

A beat.

HARRY Our Darren and Tracey have gone up to Blue Haven he sez!

DOT Again?

HARRY I said it was cheaper than getting married anyway so...

DOT Another bloody holiday?

HARRY Cheaper than being at home he says, he says he's on about renting his house out.

DOT How can he, he already rents it?

HARRY That's what he said!

DOT I wonder what he's been smoking then?

HARRY Nowt, I've given him!

A beat.

Let him buy his own!

A beat.

DOT He's a bloody nightmare that lad always has been, and she's three sheets to t' wind!

HARRY She's put some weight and all!

DOT She's pregnant again!

HARRY Is she?

DOT I can't believe you've got rid of t' ladder?

A beat.

HARRY Aye I just saw it and I thought bollocks I'm getting shut!

A beat.

DOT So what's the big plan now then?

HARRY Sommat'll turn up, I'm going to go down to t' dole office see what's what?

DOT Aye because you can't move for job offers down there, there was a bloody queue a mile long down there this morning!

HARRY Sommat'll turn up!

A beat.

DOT Aye counting bananas at Geest. Joan Scott told me that's all there is, and they only pay peanuts, and you know what you get, if you pay peanuts! This is cash in hand, you dope, that's why I suggested it!

HARRY Chris sez they're letting 'em build all sorts up on that land opposite dole office, he sez 'Council are selling the land cheap because of the strike.'

DOT Somebody'll be making a killing; it's not all council land is it?

HARRY He sez there'll be ton o jobs up there!

DOT Aye wi' no over time and shit pay!

HARRY Well that's what Chris sez!

A beat.

DOT And so that's it with the window cleaning is it?

HARRY Hadn't you had enough; walking about, people looking at you like you're a frigging Gypo or sommat?

DOT At least we worked for ussens!

HARRY You don't get it!

DOT 'Course I get it, how the frigging hell are we going to keep the lights on?

HARRY Well I'm not going into t' redundancy!

DOT We don't when we'll need it, we've wedding to pay for...

HARRY What, our Darren, we're notating for him are we?

DOT Well what about our Tina, do you think she's going be at home forever?

HARRY Our Tina's alrate just yet!

A beat.

DOT She'll be gone before you know it!

HARRY I bloody hope not, not our Tina!

DOT *is upset.*

DOT Everything's bloody changing, our Pauline, mi Dad and now my Mam's not so good!

A beat.

HARRY Why what's up wi' her?

DOT She's had to have t' doctor to her last neet, keeps going dizzy she sez!

HARRY Mind you I'd be going dizzy living with your Mam, she talks such shite, I don't know how your Dad lived with her!

A beat.

DOT I'm going to have get another job!

HARRY You'll kill your chuffing self you will.

DOT Jeeee…

　A beat.

HARRY I thought I was doing you a favour.

DOT What selling t' ladder?

HARRY It's not about selling it though is it, it's about what it sez…

DOT It sez we'd got an income that's what it

HARRY Hey…

　A beat.

　We're together!

　A beat.

DOT Are we?

HARRY Well aren't we?

　A beat.

DOT Just.

　DOT *exits,* **HARRY** *remains by the gate.*

　Music swells.*

　Lights fade.

　Black out.

---

* A licence to produce *Shafted!* does not include a performance licence for any third-party or copyrighted recordings. Licensees should create their own.

Scene Nine

*As the lights come up we see **HARRY** slumped by the garden gate, he is clearly pissed, he tries to get up but can hardly bring himself to his feet.*

Caption.

UPTON. 1993.

*After awhile **DOT** enters, she is dressed with a work smock which indicates she has a job in a warehouse. She sees **HARRY** and stops in her tracks.*

DOT 'S going off here?

HARRY Must have dropped off!

DOT At 'gate?

HARRY Time is it?

A beat.

DOT You been smoking?

HARRY *tries to stir himself.*

HARRY I can't get up!

DOT Have you been smoking that rubbish?

HARRY I've not touched it!

A beat.

DOT Get up!

HARRY I seh; him next door's got hissen a window cleaning round he sez, he's making that bloody ladder pay he sez!!

A beat.

I saw him go past this morning; he was going down Station Road at Ackworth, he says he can make a bloody mint down there!

A beat.

DOT Get up?

HARRY I think my legs have gone!

A beat.

DOT Your bloody brain's gone if you ask me!

HARRY *tries to move himself.*

HARRY Giz a lift then!

DOT *just watches him.*

DOT Get up!

HARRY I can't!

DOT *goes to him and he reeks of alcohol.*

DOT What you been drinking?

HARRY Just had a couple o cans!

DOT Of what?

HARRY Chris put me on to it; eight cans for a two quid!

DOT What is it?

HARRY I've had nowt to eat, that's why it's got me!

DOT You stink!

HARRY Felt a bit dizzy so I came out and t' heat must have got to me… I mean I used to drink pints…

A beat.

Dunno what's happened there, and suddenly I'm on mi arse! Hey I saw a Police car go passed twice but they didn't stop! Bastards!

A beat.

I waved at 'em but…

A beat.

Hey, they've got Roy Mason looking into jobs for the regeneration, regeneration they call it, I was reading about it, regeneration, Giza job Roy eh? Yosser Hughes...remember him, we thought it was all made up, didn't we?

DOT You're a disgrace!

HARRY I know that cock. Margaret Thatcher told me that!

HARRY *tries to get up off the floor, it's an effort.*

DOT Get up!

HARRY I'm trying to get bloody up!

DOT Get up?

HARRY Gi' up shouting!

DOT Get up!

HARRY Giza hand then!

DOT No!

HARRY Be rate!

DOT Get up you stinking pig!

DOT *exits through the garden gate and off stage.* **HARRY** *tries to get to his feet, it is funny and pathetic.*

HARRY Aren't we bloody well?

He struggles to stand, but is all over the place. He calls to **DOT** *offstage.*

I'm up cockl

I'm up... I'm all over t' shop...but I'm up!!

HARRY *makes his way off stage as...*

Music swells[*].

Lights fade.

Black out.

---

[*] A licence to produce *Shafted!* does not include a performance licence for any third-party or copyrighted recordings. Licensees should create their own.

Scene Ten

As the lights come up **DOT** *enters, she has a case with her
and is wearing a smart light weight summer coat, she puts
down her case and opens the gate, she is clearly upset but
can't stand this domestic hell.*

Caption.

UPTON. 1994.

As she wrestles with the gate **HARRY** *enters with a beer
and in his underpants, he is clearly beside himself with
drink and finds* **DOT***'s action incredible.*

HARRY You doing?

DOT 'It look like?

HARRY Time is it?

DOT Time you got yourself sorted out!

HARRY What's up naa?

DOT You!

HARRY What?

DOT I'm going!

HARRY Where?

DOT Down to mi Mam's!

    A beat.

HARRY Thought she was badly?

DOT Well I can't stop here!

    A beat.

HARRY What's up naa?

DOT Go out some pants on!

HARRY No!

DOT I can't stand this!

HARRY What's up naa?

DOT You, you bloody idiot!

HARRY One argument!

DOT What?

HARRY One argument and you're walking out like a big kid!

DOT One argument? Look at us. Look at what's happening, we're on the bloody edge, look at you, look at your behaviour, it's not normal it's not what normal people do. We're living on fresh air! I've got two jobs now, two jobs and that's not enough to keep us going, and will you touch the redundancy will you bloody hell.

HARRY Because when it's gone it's gone!

DOT And we'll be gone and all and have seen sod all for it!

HARRY Do you think it's a lot of money eighteen thousand? Good grief it's nowt, it's an insult, we've got that to live on for the rest of our lives! What are we supposed to do when it's gone, invent the frigging wheel?

A beat.

DOT Go and put some trousers on!

HARRY No.

DOT Yes!

HARRY The other week I was in the market cafe and I heard this woman say; all that money the miners got! And I sez, there were lads who had been at t' pit no more than a year who got next to nowt, and a bloke my age only walked away with eighteen thousand and a chest full of shit! And she sez well what about Scargill? And I says you silly sod, what about Norman Parkinson? He was knobbing half his constituency and nobody gave a toss about that! Scargill tried to fight for jobs and he's bleeding well castrated in public.

A beat.

DOT Go and out some pants on!

HARRY No!

A beat.

DOT Go and get bloody dressed!

HARRY Bollocks to getting dressed!

DOT Yes!

HARRY And bollocks to you and all, and bollocks to him next door, he's bought a fucking van now with his name on it! Tony's window cleaning! Who's he think he is?

A beat.

DOT Jesus!

Silence.

HARRY One argument and you're walking out? I thought we were better than that!

A beat.

DOT One argument?

A beat.

HARRY Well, one a day!

A beat.

DOT I can't go on like this, I can't go on living like this, how can we?

DOT *starts to become emotional.*

Do they know what they've done? Do they actually know what they've done?

A beat.

HARRY They've no idea cocka!

DOT I mean look at Colin and Jean in Askern he's not been out
of the house since strike...

A beat.

HARRY Well, he didn't go out much anyway did he, in truth.

DOT Why are you so contrary?

HARRY I'm not!

DOT He's not been out of the house since t' strike!

A beat.

It's just killing!

A beat.

And look at our Pauline, look what our Pauline did!

A beat.

HARRY Bloody hell!

DOT After Tommy left her, she had nothing, and that's what I'm
scared of, I'm scared of us having nothing!

A beat.

And you: stood in your frigging underpants arguing, and like
a bloody idiot the only chance we had you threw away coz
you didn't like cleaning windows!

A beat.

HARRY You tell me what I'm supposed to do, all my life there
was nothing but the pit! I had interest in stuff, but it was
the only option: do you think I wouldn't like to do sommat,
start again?

A beat.

She's taken my life, she's taken the lives of all my mates, she's taken the villages and shit on 'em; and if you think they haven't, you're living in a chuffing bubble!

A beat.

When they shut Frickley they took my life!

A beat.

They took my life when they shut Upton Dot, and then the bastards did it again!

A beat.

DOT Go put some trousers on!

HARRY No!

A beat.

DOT Yes!

Silence.

HARRY What can I say...

DOT How about sorry?

A beat.

HARRY For what?

DOT For never doing what the chuffing hell I tell you?

HARRY You love me for that!

DOT Do I?

DOT *walk passed* **HARRY** *with her bag and back into the house and off stage.* **HARRY** *looks to where she has exited.*

HARRY Well don't you?

A beat.

You're back then are you?

A beat.

I seh: are you back then?

Music swells.*

Lights fade.

Black out.

---

* A licence to produce *Shafted!* does not include a performance licence for any third-party or copyrighted recordings. Licensees should create their own.

Scene Eleven

Lights come up and **DOT** *is sweeping the pathway to the gate, as she gets to the gate she stops and has a moment. She looks out and then finally to the audience, this is the first time she has broken the fourth wall.*

Caption.

UPTON. 1995.

DOT He sez leave it, he sez don't be sweeping up all the time, but I can't leave it, I can't just lie down and let 'em walk all over us; I've told him, have some pride. Have some fight in yer, where's it gone?

A beat.

They've broken him, they've broken a lot of 'em on this estate!

A beat.

I mean is there any wonder?

A beat.

They were taking on an army, they were, I was there, I saw it! I was chased by police horses, what part of that did they think was fair and proper?

A beat.

They have, they've broken him!

A beat.

During strike he was like a man possessed, I mean who'd tek him on, eighteen stone of man made muscle?

A beat.

Collier fit is what he used to say: "I'm collier fit, my back, shoulders and arms, I was made at Frickley pit!" That's what he used to say!

A beat.

I just get on, you have to, keep swimming is what my Mam says: and I do, after I lost mi Dad, I just put me head down, and then there was our Pauline...

A beat.

Thing is, I don't know how long I can keep swimming for! I mean... I've got two jobs now, one at market cafe down Elmsall, and the other one at Asda!

A beat.

And our Tina's got a boyfriend now, so that's all change!

A beat.

I mean at least our Tina's got her hairdressing so that's sommat, but nobody's got a clue if she'll be able to make a go of it!

A beat.

I always fancied hairdressing, you know sommat different!

A beat.

He's been down to see Doctor Diggle, he's put him on these tablets for his nerves. He says, he'd have been better smoking pot than taking them bloody smarties!

A beat.

I've said, he needs to get hissen turned around; and then he goes off about the fact that the north will never be the same again, they've destroyed what we had, he sez! They've ripped the arsehole out of it, he says, all t' north...it'll never get turned round in a generation!

A beat.

If I could wave a magic wand and change it all back I would!

A beat.

I would... If I was a magician I'd change it all back to like it wa'.

A beat.

Coz I look at him and I wonder what's happening, I do, I just wonder what's happening to us!

Music swells.

Lights fade.

Black out.

---

* A licence to produce *Shafted!* does not include a performance licence for any third-party or copyrighted recordings. Licensees should create their own.

Scene Twelve

HARRY *enters in a pair of brightly coloured summer shorts and a dappled effect covers the stage, he wears a vest and has a hose / watering can with him, he spends some time watering the white roses downstage left and downstage right. He seems calmer than we have seen him before but there is still a strongly brooding danger about him.*

Caption.

UPTON. 1996.

After a whole **DOT** *enters, she is smoking and she is wearing summer clothes, the atmosphere is much more lyrical and gentle.*

HARRY These are coming on!

A beat.

My Dad gave me the bulbs, can you remember?

A beat.

Mind you he was no gardener wa' my Dad, he used to cut the privets and he couldn't see owt with his hay fever, they were his pride and joy and when he cut 'em he couldn't even bloody see 'em!

A beat.

Mind you our Tina's like that isn't she, how she manages in that hairdressers with all that hair about is a bloody miracle to me!

A beat.

It's a wonder she's not coughing her bloody guts up!

A beat.

DOT Headstone should be ready by next weekend according to Janet down Elmsall!

A beat.

HARRY They have to let the soil settle, it wa' t' same wi my Mam 'n Dad!

A beat.

DOT She never wanted cremating!

HARRY Lovely these roses!

DOT She never went t' doctor, mi Mam, did she, not like your Mam, she lived there, I mean she was never ill was she?

A beat.

I mean she was never ill and then she's not here, frightening how quick!

HARRY It'll be us two next!

DOT Makes you think!

HARRY I think that a cat's been on here from next door.

DOT You know...if you're doing right thing?

HARRY You should be on these tablets I'm on, they'd make you think!

A beat.

DOT What do they make you think then?

HARRY They'd make you think: I wish I wasn't on these bloody tablets!

A beat.

DOT Warm out here!

HARRY Nice little garden now this!

DOT My Mam used to say we we should get away!

A beat.

HARRY Ar?

A beat.

DOT That's what she said.

HARRY Oh ar!

DOT Well now our Tina's gone...

HARRY She's only darn Kirkby, not gone so far as she...she pops up everyday!

A beat.

Mind you she's got a right drip there with Chris's lad. They reckon he could have gone to grammar school, but to look at him he's like a wet to me!

DOT I wouldn't mind having a change.

A beat.

HARRY Ah?

DOT Do sommat!

A beat.

HARRY They reckon they're building sommat up by t' Barnsley Oak naar, so there might be sommat up there?

A beat.

DOT No I meant sommat different.

A beat.

HARRY Sommat different to what?

A beat.

DOT Sommat different to living round here!

A beat.

HARRY Why, what's up wi round here?

DOT I just fancy doing sommat, you know…you lose your Mam and…

HARRY Well ar…

A beat.

DOT I always fancied Brid!

HARRY Well we could always go for a couple of days. Where was it we used to go, that one on Marine Drive wasn't it?

DOT Sunny Side!

HARRY Sunny Side!

DOT I can't remember when it was ever sunny?

A beat.

HARRY I saw Big Daddy and Giant Haystacks in Brid, with my Grandad!

A beat.

And that wasn't yesterday!

A beat.

DOT I dunno, I've always fancied it!

HARRY Well we could have a long weekend!

A beat.

DOT Well, I was thinking of sommat a bit longer!

HARRY What, a week?

DOT Well…

HARRY A bloody week in Brid?

DOT Well I've always fancied longer than a week!

HARRY Well I'm not going to Brid for longer than a week!

A beat.

DOT Well I've always fancied sommat more...

HARRY What?

DOT Well... I?

A beat.

HARRY What, you mean to live there?

A beat.

DOT Well...

HARRY ...and do what?

A beat.

DOT I always fancied having my own place!

HARRY What a flat?

A beat.

DOT Well a B and B!

A beat.

HARRY A B and B?

A beat.

DOT Yes!

HARRY What, a boarding house?

DOT Well...that's what a B and B is!

A beat.

HARRY Well how could we afford to buy a boarding house?

A beat.

DOT Well we could sell this!

HARRY Oh right!

DOT I think we could get twenty thousand for it!

HARRY Oh right!

A beat.

DOT And then there's that little bit mi Mam left me!

HARRY Oh right!

DOT And we could take some of t' redundancy…couldn't we?

A beat.

Be nice that, I think; a new start, I mean what with everything that went off wi t' strike. I mean, you know, me getting involved and all that, I mean I've worked in a kitchen haven't I so…

A beat.

HARRY Oh right then!

A beat.

DOT Don't you think?

HARRY Don't I think what?

A beat.

DOT That we should have a change?

A beat.

HARRY Eh?

DOT Don't you think?

Silence.

HARRY Well I'm going nowhere!

DOT Well…

HARRY I'm staying here, you go, this is where I'm stopping!

A beat.

DOT Well don't you...

A beat.

HARRY I'm staying here.

DOT But...

HARRY I'm staying here!

A beat.

You go if you want!

A beat.

This is my home, this is where I belong.

A beat.

You can't just up and off, you daft get!

A beat.

That's what they want us to do, to have no belonging, they want to weaken us, so it doesn't matter who we are, or where we live! They want everywhere to be like everywhere else, so they can transport us and use us like a bloody commodity! We've got roots!

DOT I know that!

HARRY That's what it means, it means we're connected to the bloody soil you silly sod!

DOT It's only Brid, it's not fifty miles away!

HARRY Well if you want to go, go: get, piss off...this is where I belong!

DOT But there's nowt here for us now, open your eyes!

HARRY There is for me!

DOT It's over, it's finished, open your bloody eyes, there's nothing here anymore, it's gone forever and they'll never get it back!

Open your bloody eyes! We've done all we can, we've given it a go, but it's killing us, it's killing everybody, that's what they've done to us, they've bloody turned the oxygen off! Can't you bloody see that you stubborn get!

DOT *storms off stage.*

HARRY *is aggressively angry and screams at the top of his voice.*

HARRY Well I'm going bloody nowhere, I'm staying here!

A beat.

I'm bloody staying here!

Music swells.*

Lights fade.

Black out.

---

* A licence to produce *Shafted!* does not include a performance licence for any third-party or copyrighted recordings. Licensees should create their own.

ACT II

Scene Thirteen

House lights fade.

HARRY *enters with* **DOT** *in a wheelchair, he is seventy-five and she is in her late sixties.* **DOT** *is suffering from a brain tumour and is miserable but still funny. As* **HARRY** *enters with her in the wheelchair he positions her centrally and she adjusts herself.*

Caption.

UPTON. 2014.

HARRY It's cold out here!

DOT It's not that bad!

HARRY Bloody freezing!

DOT It's them tablets you're on. You've got blood like water!

HARRY Well I'm on water tablets, that'll be why!

DOT That's why you're cold all the time!

A beat.

HARRY Let me get you to t' car then!

DOT It's like a bloody wrestling match getting me in't car! You're wheezing like an old man!

HARRY I've two lungs full o shit that's why!

DOT Like a bloody barrel organ squeaking!

HARRY We should've kept the van, that would've been easier, I could have just dumped you in the back. You ready then?

HARRY *moves to shift the wheelchair.*

DOT Hang on, let me just have a minute, you're always rushing me!

HARRY I'm not!

DOT You're always bullying me!

HARRY I'm not!

DOT You bloody are!

HARRY Well if I am I'm only getting my own back!

DOT How are you?

HARRY Well you've bullied me for long enough!

DOT I haven't!

A beat.

HARRY You bloody have!

A beat.

DOT I thought I was going to faint when I was in with t' consultant!

HARRY Aye he likes it warm.

DOT Nice shoes and all!

HARRY Ar?

DOT I seh, he had nice shoes did that Cancer Doctor!

HARRY I didn't look at his bloody shoes!

DOT Well you never do, you never have done: you can judge a man by his shoes; never notice anything you! It could be throwing it down and you'd never notice!

A beat.

No, he had nice shoes! Expensive!

HARRY Well I bet he can afford them can't he, with what they charge! Free at the point of entry, but if you want owt else it'll cost you a bloody kidney!

DOT Oh we're off!

HARRY Mind you they're doing what they can, and I reckon they're doing alright with our Darren.

A beat.

DOT Oh ar there's that!

HARRY Oh ar.

A beat.

DOT I think we'll have a run out to the Mining Museum up at Caphouse, just to pass an hour!

HARRY When?

DOT Now?

HARRY Again?

DOT Aye I think well have a run up there: and I'll have a Magnum!

HARRY Eh?

DOT I seh, I'll have a Magnum?

HARRY I thought you weren't suppose to eat owt creamy?

DOT Oh shut up you!

A beat.

HARRY Well I'm not taking you for a Magnum!

DOT I thought you like t' Mining Museum?

HARRY I do, but I'm not taking you for a Magnum! You're not suppose to eat cream stuff 'Doctor said!

DOT Oh shut up you!

HARRY That's what Doctor said!!

DOT Well I fancy one, so I'm having one!

A beat.

HARRY What a bloody carry on with you…

A beat.

DOT Are you going to take me for a Magnum then or what?

HARRY No!

DOT You bloody are!

HARRY *starts to position himself to steer the wheelchair.*

HARRY There you go again!

DOT What?

HARRY Bullying!

DOT Oh shut up!

HARRY That's verbal abuse is that! You can be arrested for that!

DOT Well you should've been arrested years ago then!

HARRY And you should!

HARRY *repositions himself with the wheelchair.*

DOT And you should!

HARRY Verbal abuse they call it!

DOT Oh shit you!

HARRY And now we're swearing?

DOT Shit to you!

HARRY Lovely that!

DOT Shit!

HARRY Absolutely bloody lovely!

A beat.

DOT You'll miss me when I'm not here!

HARRY You think I will!

DOT You will!

HARRY I'll be alright! I'll get somebody else!

DOT You won't!

HARRY I will!

DOT Who?

HARRY Ah well…

A beat.

DOT Come on you silly sod, take me up to Caphouse and I'll have a Magnum!

HARRY And that's mental abuse that! They'd lock you up in a prison if I told anybody what you'd done to me over the last fifty years.

DOT Good, go and tell 'em, put me out of my bloody misery!

HARRY I would and all!

DOT I know you would, you're bloody hateful!

A beat.

HARRY A Magnum then?

DOT It's bloody freezing out here!

HARRY What do you want a Magnum for then?

DOT Oh shut up, and get me to the Mining Museum before they close that down and all!

HARRY Oh you!

DOT Come on, let's tek the bastards on again!

HARRY You're bloody funny you.

DOT I'm not being bloody funny, come on!

*As **HARRY** wheels her off stage slowly the two of them laugh at their banter.*

Music swells[*].

Lights fade.

Black out.

---

* A licence to produce *Shafted!* does not include a performance licence for any third-party or copyrighted recordings. Licensees should create their own.

Scene Fourteen

It is evening. **HARRY** *enters in the same costume underdressed that we have seen him in from the top of Act II although he is now wearing a paper party hat since he is at a Turkey and Tinsel event at a hotel on the South Coast.*

Caption.

EASTBOURNE. 2010.

DOT *enters in a smart Marks and Spencer's outfit, she has a streamer around her neck and she also wears a paper hat.*

DOT You're out here then, are you?

HARRY I've come out of the bloody way!

A beat.

DOT What're you playing at?

HARRY He was getting on my bloody nerves!

DOT Why do you have to spoil everything?

HARRY It was him!

DOT Well you kept going on!

HARRY He started it, telling me he'd been in the bloody Police!

DOT Well there was no need to go for him!

HARRY Going on about all the bloody overtime he got during t' strike?

DOT It was thirty years ago.

HARRY Twenty-six!

DOT Oh, well let it go!

HARRY Let it go? I can't let it go, I can't sit there with him going on about the aggro they caused and him laughing all the way to the bloody bank!

DOT Bloody embarrassing!

A beat.

HARRY He hadn't got a bloody clue, because he wasn't there.

DOT Oh here we go!

HARRY Well!

DOT We're at a bloody Christmas party for God's sake! We're on a bus trip!

A beat.

I mean the bloody bus shook me to bits and then you start launching into a rant about t' strike!

HARRY Well...

DOT It's history now!

HARRY Not to me it's not!

DOT It'll kill you!

HARRY It's what made me, it's what made the north. And I'll tell you this...

DOT ...I mean my turkey was tough enough, but with you going on...

HARRY The north hasn't got over it even now!

DOT Stuck in my teeth some of it...

HARRY It's never got over t' strike!

DOT And when you started thumping the table there was pigs in blankets jumping about all over the bloody shop, her next to me looked like she was having a panic do!

A beat.

HARRY Aye well...sorry about that!

DOT Where did you think you were?

A beat.

HARRY I knew I wasn't going to like him when we got on his table!

DOT Well how did you know that then?

HARRY Well he's got all his hair for a start; I mean how come he's got a full head of hair at seventy? I'll tell you why, he's never had any muck in it; he's never had to bloody wash it, that's why! And when he told me that he'd been in the Met, I thought, oh look out!

A beat.

DOT I thought you'd calmed down but...

A beat.

HARRY I shouldn't've grabbed him, that was wrong... I admit that!

A beat.

And I didn't know that he'd got a bad heart otherwise I'd have left him!

DOT 'You've got angina!

A beat.

HARRY He was alright once he'd taken his spray wasn't he?

DOT It was bloody shocking when you threw him to the floor!

HARRY He tripped up there!

DOT He "hell as like" tripped up!!

HARRY Hey, I was a ripper, if somebody criticises t' miners they're criticising my reason for being.

DOT I thought they were going to call t' Police!

HARRY Hey didn't need to did they, he was in't Police! That'll teach him not to mess about wi't miners!

A beat.

DOT You've not been a miner since 1984. They got shut of 'em all! You've not been near a pit for years?

A beat.

HARRY I have!

DOT You bloody haven't!

A beat.

HARRY I go to the Mining Museum!

DOT It's not the same!

A beat.

HARRY It is to me!

A beat.

DOT We should've asked to be moved to them on that table from Hull, they were all ex-trawler men, they seemed to be having a good time, and we get stuck with somebody who'd be in the bloody Met!

HARRY In fact I thought I'd seen his face before!

DOT Give up!

HARRY I'd seen him before, I'm telling you!

DOT I thought he didn't know what he was talking about coz he wasn't there?

HARRY I bet he was at Orgreave?

DOT Eh?

HARRY I bet he was!

DOT How can he have been, if he wasn't there?

HARRY I bet he was at Orgreave, now then!

DOT He was never!

HARRY I never forget a face?

DOT Well that's a miracle because you forget everything bloody else...

A beat.

Well we can't go back in there now, not with all that pull-aver!

A beat.

HARRY Did they call for an ambulance then or...?

DOT There was a doctor at the Rotary "do" in the other room apparently, once they'd brought him back round, he seemed alright!

A beat.

HARRY He'll be alrate, mind you, it'll be one Christmas he'll not forget in a bloody hurry!

DOT Oh aye!

HARRY He'd have wished he'd never opened his bloody mouth about miners' strike?

DOT He will and all!

A beat.

HARRY He'll have wished that he never ever met me!

DOT He will!

HARRY He will and all!

DOT He will!

A beat.

And he'll not be by himself there will he?

HARRY *coughs heavily.* **DOT** *can't ignore it.*

HARRY What do you mean by that?

A beat.

I seh, what do you mean by that?

DOT You're an embarrassment; getting yourself all worked up!

HARRY Hey, I only bite if I'm attacked!

DOT Well what about that woman who'd just got an Open University degree, ninety-one she was and you had a go at her first!

HARRY'*s coughing subsides.*

HARRY Well she was talking bloody rubbish and all!

DOT It had taken her forty-five years to get a degree in Modern History, and I tell you this she knew what she was talking about!

HARRY Well there's no wonder is there, she's lived through most of it!

A beat.

DOT Why don't go in there and apologise?

HARRY *is annoyed.*

HARRY For what?

DOT For grabbing him!

HARRY He wanted bloody grabbing!

HARRY *shouts at* **DOT.**

DOT Who are you shouting at?

HARRY *has to calm himself, it has become calmer, though coughs again.*

HARRY I'll go and apologise then.

DOT Why don't you?

A beat.

HARRY Though what I'm apologising for, is a bloody mystery to me!

A beat.

DOT It'll show you're the bigger man!

A beat.

HARRY But I'll tell you this, if he chelps back at me, I'll bloody well hit him, bad heart or not, I'm telling you that for nowt!

HARRY *exits unhappily.*

DOT Merry Christmas by the way!

Music swells.*

Lights fade.

Black out.

---

* A licence to produce *Shafted!* does not include a performance licence for any third-party or copyrighted recordings. Licensees should create their own.

Scene Fifteen

It is evening. **DOT** *remains on stage, she takes an indigestion tablet from her hand bag, and pops it in her mouth, she is clearly anxious as she wanders around the space. She is outside an hospital and is waiting for the results of* **HARRY**'*s heart attack.*

Caption.

UPTON. 2004.

She chews on her indigestion tablet and then looks to get out a packet of cigarettes, though she doesn't light up.

DOT You can't tell him owt, never been able to, all his life he's been the same, if you say it's black, he'll say it's white, if you say it's Tuesday, he'll swear to God it's Wednesday, why would you be so bloody contrary?

And now this, a bloody heart attack!

A beat.

I've said to him, you'll have a bloody heart attack you will, but he never bloody listens! Gets hissen all worked up over what's happened and we can't do owt about it!

A beat.

And with what he eats, is there any bloody wonder?

A beat.

We went on a cruise wi P and O and he ate like there was no tomorrow.

A beat.

I told him three years ago that we needed a pet, so the silly sod bought three carp for t' pond at t' back!

A beat.

I said to him you can't walk a fish; he said, I know, that's why I bought them!

A beat.

Mind you it's only his first, I mean his brother had nine!

A beat.

Heart attacks, not fish, he didn't like fish to be honest, well I don't think he did!

A beat.

I mean who has nine heart attacks?

A beat.

Well his brother did, their Eric: he didn't want to go home from hospital after they discharged him for the ninth time, because he couldn't bare living in an house where she didn't tidy up; so he ran around the ward until he had another, killed hissen running round the ward!

A beat.

And when we were in't ambulance, all he's asking is; have the Paramedics got a decent pay deal, have they got any overtime in? What's their conditions of service?

A beat.

He's bloody obsessed with it: and the silly sods, are talking to him like he's Tony Benn.

A beat.

I mean, to be honest I've felt off it for a couple of months, I have since we moved into t' bungalow, but I can't be poorly now there's sommat wrong with him!

A beat.

I think a lot of this is with what's happened with our Darren! And I've teld him: 'That's not doing your Dad any good, that! All that's not helping your Dad at all!'

A beat.

And then there's our Tina's job! When her business went through the floor, we wanted to help her and Martin, I mean that's why we let it go! And he sez that's all to do with the strike!

A beat.

You can't tell him to slow down gets all worked up, only forty-seven percent of them jobs have been replaced he says, he's like a bull in a bloody china shop, he gets himself all strung up because of it!

A beat.

I've teld him, you'll be dead before you're sixty-five if you don't calm yourself.

A beat.

He's a pigging nuisance at times! He is: a pigging bloody nuisance!

Music swells.*

Lights fade.

Black out.

---

* A licence to produce *Shafted!* does not include a performance licence for any third-party or copyrighted recordings. Licensees should create their own.

Scene Sixteen

It is day time. **DOT** *remains on stage as* **HARRY** *enters! She grabs baggage from upstage. He is dressed slightly less formally but still relatively smart. He is sixty-four and carries with him two large suitcases.* **DOT** *is emotional at leaving the enterprise she set her heart and soul on.*

Caption.

BRIDLINGTON. 2003.

HARRY Everything's on the lorry, so do you want to come with me, or do you want to ride with the stuff?

DOT Well I don't want to be with the stuff do I? What makes you think I want to be riding in the bloody lorry with all them lads stinking of sweat? You do come out with some rubbish at times!

HARRY I'm only asking, I don't know what you want to do!

DOT I don't really want to be selling up again to be honest and going back to bloody Upton, if you want to know the truth.

HARRY Well it's a bit late for that now, 'lorries are all full!

DOT Have you been towing with them lads?

HARRY I've only be trying to clear the loft out!

DOT You're sweating, you'll end up badly you will.

HARRY Give up woman, I'm collier fit!

DOT You think you are!

HARRY I'm fitter that half of these wet rags on here!

A beat.

DOT Do you think we'll sell it?

HARRY We'll sell it, I mean we might have to give it away, but…!

A beat.

DOT I did think that once we've sold up and got settled we could go on a cruise me and you!

HARRY Eh?

DOT A cruise!

A beat.

HARRY Whatever for?

DOT Well, I've always fancied a cruise!

HARRY A bloody cruise, they're full of arseholes!

DOT How do you know?

HARRY A bloody cruise, they're full of retired policemen and teachers: what would you want to do a cruise for? Stuck on a boat with a load of arseholes, I'd rather drown myself?

DOT Well you can jump off then, can't you?

A beat.

HARRY I would do!

DOT You should do!

A beat.

HARRY A bloody cruise now?

DOT How do you know owt about who goes on cruises?

HARRY Well they are!

DOT How do you know?

HARRY Well they just are!

DOT How do you know?

HARRY Well you want us to go on one so they must be!

Silence.

DOT I can't believe we're just packing up and leaving? Five years just gone like that!

HARRY Hey, we're only doing what anybody else would do for their kids, helping out with 'money?

DOT After all the bloody heartache!

A beat.

HARRY Well we're going home, just think about it like that!

DOT I'm thinking about it like that love, I'm thinking about why we left Upton in the first place...

A beat.

And I don't know about living in a bungalow, feels like my life is over.

A beat.

...feels like it's going to rake everything up again!

HARRY Hey, there's all new developments there now, they've had all that European money, they're opening that Xscape place soon, anyway we'll be able to keep more of an eye on our Darren!

DOT That's a disaster that is, bloody drugs... I never thought I'd live to see that!

HARRY It happens!

DOT It didn't happen to you, did it?

HARRY Well I had you didn't I, telling me what a silly sod I was! I mean that Tracey's a bigger dope head than him! She smokes more than him, our Tina teld me!

DOT And the kiddies?

HARRY I could slap the bloody lot of 'em!

DOT Oh leave that now!

HARRY I could handle that bloody lot of dope heads, don't worry about that!

A beat.

DOT They're up at her mother's most of the time! So goodness knows what they're getting up to!

HARRY I don't know what he ever saw in her?

DOT And I don't want you over doing it when we get back, I don't want you getting yourself worked up when we go down to see him!

HARRY I could still teach our Darren a lesson!

DOT You're nearly sixty-five you silly sod, give it a miss!

A beat.

HARRY Right, come on move yourself, we've to get all this in storage then I'm back tonight to let somebody have a look around tomorrow.

HARRY *stands with the cases,* **DOT** *remains still on stage. She is upset and begins to cry quite distressingly, she slowly makes her way off stage as...*

DOT I don't know if I coming or going at the minute... And I'm sure there's sommat wrong with me you know?

HARRY It's your nerves, isn't it!

HARRY *exits.*

DOT I don't think it is my nerves, I think it might be sommat else to be honest, I've got a funny feeling you know, but I don't think it is my nerves!

Music swells.*

Lights fade.

Black out.

---

* A licence to produce *Shafted!* does not include a performance licence for any third-party or copyrighted recordings. Licensees should create their own.

Scene Seventeen

Caption.

BRIDLINGTON 1998.

HARRY *enters in summer shirt and carries a bottle of Cava which has been opened and two glasses.* **DOT** *remains on stage from the previous scene.*

HARRY Nice out here!

DOT It's a nice night!

HARRY Quiet and all, for a change!

DOT 'Been barmy hasn't it?

HARRY All bloody season!

A beat.

DOT I'm absolutely buggered!

HARRY *offers her a drink.*

HARRY 'You want one?

DOT Just a taste!

HARRY Fantastic this!

HARRY *puts her a glass of Cava.*

DOT Is it champagne?

HARRY It's Cava, calm down!

DOT *takes a drink.*

DOT Here's to your first soufflé then!

HARRY Aye, it's taken me two years to get it right but...

DOT And to your quiche!

HARRY Which was burnt!

DOT I noticed that!

HARRY But they ate it!

DOT I noticed that and all!

HARRY I was sweating like a bloody racehorse cooking that!

DOT And your Yorkshires are passable! At last!

HARRY Passable, they're my piece de resistance!

A beat.

DOT First weekend off in two bloody years!

HARRY It's harder than pit work is this!

A beat.

DOT Funny though isn't it?

HARRY What?

A beat.

DOT Dunno, I just think it's been a bit awkward at times!

HARRY Cooking that soufflé was bloody awkward I'll tell you that much!

A beat.

DOT No, you know, with some of them!

A beat.

HARRY Well we're doing uz best!

A beat.

DOT You know especially with folks who've come from home!

HARRY Well...

DOT Didn't you get that?

A beat.

HARRY They're alright, aren't they?

A beat.

DOT I just thought they were a bit...

HARRY What?

DOT You know, the fact that we're making a go of it!

HARRY Well...

DOT I mean it's not like we're running the Ritz is it?

HARRY Well...

HARRY *has another drink of Cava.*

DOT I just got a feeling, especially with them from Upton!

HARRY Well ar but...

DOT You know, who did we think we are, sort of thing?

HARRY *drinks the Cava.*

HARRY Well that's people isn't it?

DOT And she'd only come to have a look, had't she, Joan Scott?

HARRY Well ar but...

DOT She'd only come to pry!

HARRY Well ar...

DOT And Jeff Swift 'n them!

A beat.

HARRY Jeff's alright!

DOT I mean they usually go up to a caravan at Bempton cliffs, so why did they come here, just to see what's going off, that's why!

A beat.

HARRY Jeff's alright!

A beat.

DOT Put some weight on!

HARRY Jeff's alright!

A beat.

DOT It's easier wi folks you don't know though isn't it?

HARRY Jeff Swift's alright!

A beat.

DOT Jealous!

HARRY Well...

DOT I mean nobody stopped them from doing it did they?

A beat.

HARRY I think they just came for a nosey that's all!

DOT I know but they're like fish out of water aren't they?

HARRY Well Jeff's not worked since they laid him off from Next! Hey he liked my display, made him laugh that did, he said it wa't best laugh he'd had for ages.

DOT Maybe it's me then!

HARRY People are people old cock!

DOT I'll tell you this much though.

HARRY What naa?

DOT I bet they never come back!

HARRY Well...

DOT I bet they never book again!

HARRY What does it matter?

DOT So they can't have enjoyed it that much can they? They've just come to snoop on us! They must think we're bloody loaded naa!

HARRY Well compared to them...

DOT And it's a good job they haven't seen you swanning about with a bottle of bloody champagne is it?

HARRY It's not champagne, is it, it's only bloody Cava!

DOT Bloody Cava naa...

> **DOT** *exits, as* **HARRY** *finishes the bottle of Cava.*

HARRY It's a bit acidy on mi stomach but it's life in the fast lane isn't it?

Music swells.*

Lights.

Black out.

---

* A licence to produce *Shafted!* does not include a performance licence for any third-party or copyrighted recordings. Licensees should create their own.

Scene Eighteen

HARRY *enters in a pair of overalls, he is sixty-one, he has a pot of paint with him and he carries a large gnome. He takes a cloth from his pocket and starts to wipe down the gnome, cleaning it ready for painting. He blows bits from the gnome and take real pride in his work. He holds the gnome up to the sunlight so he can get a better look at his subject.*

Caption.

BRIDLINGTON. 1997.

As he prepares the gnome for its make over **DOT** *enters. She dressed in a colourful summer dress and colourful mules, she has a packet of cigarettes with her which she uses more as a prop than as a lifestyle choice.*

DOT Doin'?

HARRY 'It look like?

DOT You're painting a gnome!

HARRY It's for out at the front, near the wagon wheel!

DOT We have got other stuff to do!

HARRY I know but I wanted to get this done while it wasn't raining!

DOT Do you have to do that?

HARRY Why, what do you want me to do?

DOT There's a hundred and one things to do!

A beat.

And what happened yesterday, while I was over at our Tina's?

HARRY With what?

DOT 'That couple who left?

HARRY Nowt happened did it?

DOT Have you seen their letter?

HARRY No!

DOT It said they'd ordered an evening meal last night!

HARRY They got an evening meal last night.

DOT They said they'd got fish and chips!

HARRY Why what's up wi that?

DOT They said you went out to get it!

HARRY I did!

DOT From Busy Bees?

HARRY Why what's up with Busy Bees, it's a good fish and chip shop!

DOT I think they wanted an evening meal that we might have cooked for them, not fish and chips twice wrapped up in the paper!

HARRY Well I didn't have time to cook for 'em because I was busy!

DOT What, painting bloody gnomes?

HARRY Well they never said owt to me, and they bloody wolfed 'em down!

DOT Why didn't you just cook 'em sommat?

HARRY Because I don't like!

DOT Well didn't you think at least to take 'em out the paper, and put them on a sodding plate!

HARRY Why, what's up wi that?

DOT When I'm not here you've got to cover for me?

HARRY I did cover for you!

DOT By going to t' chip shop?

HARRY Well...

DOT You're more concerned with painting that bloody lot!

HARRY Image is everything they said at that hoteliers group!

DOT And what sort of guest house gives people their tea in a newspaper?

A beat.

Now they'll say what a bad time they've had: that's our reputation down the toilet! We've got to try with folk, not put people off, like you do!

HARRY Oh bugger 'em, they were from Grantham anyway, if they don't come back it's their own bloody look out!

DOT We're supposed to be looking after all the customers not just them who worked in the pits or on a bloody trawler, you only speak to folk who you think you're going to like!

A beat.

You're like Frankenstien's monster drifting about.

HARRY I'm not!

DOT I've seen you!

HARRY What?

DOT Vetting the bookings.

HARRY When?

DOT Last weekend, we had three phone calls from Eastbourne and they were just in the bin crumpled up! Did you think I wouldn't see them? And we've only had five bookings this week, two from Castleford, one from Hull, a couple from Wales and that bloke from Kent! And we've had none from Nottingham in all the time we've been here, so how do you work that out?

HARRY Well that's not my fault is it, maybe they all go to Skeggy?

DOT I heard you asking somebody where they were bloody born last week, so isn't that your fault either?

HARRY Hey listen...

DOT Oh don't start!

HARRY I'm playing away from home here old cock!

DOT I know that!

A beat.

And what about that woman who complained because you were stalking her in the loo!

HARRY Who?

DOT You, you silly sod!

HARRY I wasn't stalking her in the loo!

DOT She said you was!

HARRY She said somebody had left a floater and I was trying to get it sorted out for her!

HARRY *continues his painting.*

DOT I've to watch you like a bloody hawk, if we make a go of this it'll sodding well kill me!

A beat.

HARRY Well if you ask me, they're all arseholes!

DOT What the gnomes?

HARRY Featherstone-on-Sea is what I heard some woman call Brid last week! And I'm supposed to keep my mouth shut?

DOT And there's a couple into tonight from Castleford so don't start on about rugby again.

HARRY I'm going fishing toneet so you can get their fish and chips sorted!

DOT Again?

HARRY Well there's no point living in Brid and not doing is there?

A beat. **DOT** *regains some dignity.*

DOT And how many of them gnomes have you done now?

HARRY Fifty-two!

DOT Fifty-two?

HARRY What's up with that?

DOT And how much did they cost?

HARRY I got a job lot, Chris Cooper, who used to work at Frickley he's got a firm that distributes 'em, did me a deal. He sells all sorts, he's got the Blues Brothers, Marilyn Monroe, Elvis, we could have an Elvis if you want?

DOT Bloody hell!

A beat.

Elvis and some gnomes, it's not life in the fast lane is it, running a B and B with you?

HARRY He says he can get an Elvis gnome, I said I'd let him know!

A beat.

DOT Do we really need fifty-two gnomes?

HARRY Well I had to do sommat with that backyard because we're looking onto the funeral parlour, I'll get some fish in that pond and all. Get some carp in it!

DOT watches him treat the gnomes with real affection.

DOT I sometimes think you lost your way you know?

HARRY How do you mean?

DOT Your artistic skill.

HARRY concentrates on his work.

HARRY I was good at art at school.

A beat.

DOT What's happened since then?

HARRY Bugger off!

A beat.

DOT No I'll say this much for you, you've done a good job, sanding 'em down and starting from scratch, I've been impressed.

HARRY Well if a job's worth doing...

DOT No they do look good, I just didn't think we'd have the red army living with us!

A beat.

HARRY I enjoy doing 'em!

DOT I can see that!

A beat.

HARRY And I've given 'em all names!

DOT Eh?

HARRY I say I've given them all names.

DOT That's good then!

A beat.

That'll keep you busy!

HARRY Well you've got to give 'em names haven't you?

DOT Have you?

HARRY Yes, otherwise how do you know who's who?

A beat.

DOT Who are they then, Dopey, Sneezey and that?

HARRY Eh no, I've got; Parkinson, Thatcher, MacGregor, Scargill, Benn, Kinnock, Heseltine. Heaton. All characters from Miners' strike.

DOT Well it's an interesting theme anyway!

HARRY Oh aye they're all there!

DOT Who's that you're doing at the minute then?

A beat.

HARRY I don't know yet!

A beat.

It could be Gorbachev or Prince Phillip!

DOT A bit different then?

HARRY *considers the gnome.*

HARRY Or it could be Kevin Keegan when I think about it!

DOT Well when you decide who it is, go and do some washing up, and get Kevin to give you a hand!

HARRY *exits, carrying his gnome,* **DOT** *watches him go, picks up the paint he has left on stage and follows him off stage.*

HARRY I don't know if this is Kevin in all truth, looks more like a Smurf than owt else! Mind you they didn't have owt to do with t' strike though did they?

A beat.

Might have been working with the Met undercover though, tha' never knows!

A beat.

They were all a set of bastards midgets!

Music swells.*

Lights fade.

Black out.

---

* A licence to produce *Shafted!* does not include a performance licence for any third-party or copyrighted recordings. Licensees should create their own.

Scene Nineteen

DOT *enters, she has a fold out garden chair with her, she is covered in paint, and is relieved to be in the outside, she unfolds the chair and sits in it, she is exhausted.*

Caption.

BRIDLINGTON. 1996.

As she sits in the heat and relaxes **HARRY** *enters, he is wearing a vest and has a brush with him, he also wears sunglasses, it is especially warm.* **DOT** *also wears sunglasses,* **HARRY** *has a little chair and sits on it.*

DOT This is the life!

HARRY Oh ar!

DOT Lovely out here!

HARRY It's a sun trap!

DOT We'll just have an hour!

HARRY It's like the south o bloody France out here!

DOT How do you know you've never been!

   A beat.

HARRY I watch tele!

   A beat.

DOT It's bloody roasting!

HARRY Oh this is it!

DOT I'm buggered to be honest!

   A beat.

HARRY Well you're fifty-five and you're running round like somebody not right!

DOT Well time's going!

A beat.

HARRY I think it's looking good.

DOT It will be when it's finished.

A near.

HARRY Bit of an awkward outlook onto the funeral parlour at the back like but...

DOT We need something to distract from that. Can't we get some gnomes or sommat?

A beat.

HARRY Eh?

DOT I seh, get some gnomes to hide it!

A beat.

HARRY How many would we need?

DOT Well...!

HARRY You'd need bloody thousands!

DOT Well we need sommat.

HARRY We'll get a Wishing Well, it'll be rate with that.

A beat.

DOT Gnomes would be good!

HARRY Gnomes?

A beat.

DOT Be good if you got a few though?

A beat.

HARRY I'm getting no bloody gnomes.

DOT You could paint 'em and all that!

A beat.

HARRY I'm not painting a load of gnomes, hellfire what do you think I chuffing am?

A beat.

DOT Could do with something out at the front and all!

HARRY Well I'm having no gnomes out at the front, so you can bloody forget that!

A beat.

I mean there were blokes who'd shit their pants if they were on the same shift as me at t' pit, they'd mess their sen if I looked at 'em and tha' wants me to come to Brid and start painting a load of pissing gnomes, naa?

A beat.

I mean, I know I've done some bloody daft stuff, but I've still got a bit of pride, good God!

A beat.

DOT You could get one that's fishing, and stick it by the pond!

HARRY Bollocks no, I'm painting no bloody gnomes!

Silence.

DOT Do you think we've done the right thing?

HARRY What, trying to paint every room in a weekend?

DOT No I mean...

HARRY What?

DOT Well...

Silence.

HARRY Hey...

DOT What?

HARRY Wow...don't start saying that now, for God's sake don't start saying that naar?

DOT I'm only saying!

HARRY I know what you're only saying and don't, even bloody well think about it!

A beat.

DOT It's such a leap though isn't it, I didn't think it'd be such hard work!

Silence.

HARRY We can always is go back!

DOT I'll never go back.

HARRY No?

DOT I'll never go back to Upton naa, there's nowt there for me!

A beat.

HARRY What about t' kids?

DOT They're big enough to look after themselves naa, they don't need us!

A beat.

HARRY And thank God for that!

A beat.

DOT I just hope it works out, and we become the folks who lived on the hill!

A beat.

HARRY Well we've got a Boarding house that's on a bit of a hill, so it's a start!

DOT *has pains in her stomach.*

DOT I've got a right heavy feeling in my stomach!

HARRY Well there's little wonder is there, bloody crackers!

A beat.

DOT It's from living with you!

A beat.

HARRY Yes, I knew it would be my fault.

Silence.

DOT Oh come on then!

HARRY What?

DOT Back at it!

HARRY We haven't had our statuary break, have we?

DOT We have!

HARRY We haven't had a proper Union tea break though!

A beat.

DOT We're working by my rules now!

HARRY Yes I know your rules, they keep changing all the bloody time!

DOT *stands slowly, she is in some discomfort.*

DOT Oh my stomach, if it keeps on like this I might have to go and see somebody.

HARRY Have a bit of grass, might relax you!

DOT Well it didn't bloody well relax you did it, you ended up on tablets!

HARRY And I never thought that!

A beat.

DOT Come on then let's task and finish, then we can have a walk on the front and have a game of bingo! We might even win sommat!

HARRY You should've never got involved with that women's group!

DOT Come on then, slave!

HARRY I am and all, story of my life, that!

A beat.

DOT Bridlington eh? Don't you just love it?

A beat.

HARRY No, not yet I don't!

Music swells.*

Lights fade.

Black out.

---

* A licence to produce *Shafted!* does not include a performance licence for any third-party or copyrighted recordings. Licensees should create their own.

Scene Twenty

DOT *and* HARRY *reposition the garden gate in the scene change.* DOT *enters, she is fifty-four and she is wearing the costume we saw her wearing at the end of Act I, she has a suitcase with her, and is preparing to leave home, she stands at the garden gate. She has a cloth and is wiping it down the gate.*

Caption.

UPTON. 1996.

HARRY *enters, with a number of cases and is wearing a pair of casual slacks and a Fred Perry shirt, he is fifty-six and this is his smartish attire.*

DOT Alright?

A beat.

HARRY I've been better!

DOT I've just been wiping the gate down!

HARRY What for!

DOT Well...

HARRY Bloody leave it.

DOT I want to leave it clean.

A beat.

HARRY I'm surprised you haven't swept round the bloody estate, I've seen me come home from t' pit and you've been sweeping round by Johnny Brown's house.

A beat.

You need to bloody drop all that, it'll be the death of you!

DOT Our Darren said he'll come over tonight if he can, and bring the kids.

HARRY Which means we won't see him for a month!

DOT I worry about him and all that grass he smokes!

HARRY He's alright, he's not like me, he's got more sense!

DOT I've asked him to help us with some of the emulsioning, but...

HARRY Yes, for a decorator he bloody well hates painting.

A beat.

DOT He's the worse decorator I've ever seen to be honest!

HARRY And when he wallpapers you can see the joins, he starts from the wrong place, but you can't bloody say owt to him, I don't know who he bloody takes after?

A beat.

DOT And that'll have to stop and all!

HARRY What?

DOT Swearing.

A beat.

HARRY Why, don't they have swearing in Brid? It's bloody changed since I was last there, if they don't!

DOT Just...

HARRY Right, I've got the bloody message!

A beat.

DOT And our Tina'll ring us she said.

HARRY And that'll be another first!

Silence.

DOT Bloody hell you!

HARRY What's up naa?

A beat.

DOT You don't make it easy do you?

HARRY Well you know what I think...so I'm saying nowt, I could stop here, me!

A beat.

But it's too late naa, it's all done and dusted!

A beat.

DOT Well let's not get into it...

HARRY No let's just do what you say...

A beat.

DOT It's just as hard for me!

HARRY We've let this house go for nowt, I mean we were encouraged to buy and we've let it go for bloody nowt.

A beat.

DOT Like your ladder!

HARRY Shit!

A beat.

DOT She's moving and all she sez, her next door, so I don't know what'll happen on this corner! And she sez Jeff Swift's got hissen a job up at Next.

HARRY Ah, shit money and no power, they can get rid of you at the drop of a hat!

A beat.

You fart out of place up there and you're back on't dole! You even look at somebody funny and you're history, it's 'same all over! That's what they've done, they've got us where they want us!

A beat.

DOT Well they haven't got you have they, because you're going to Brid!

A beat.

HARRY Aye, the Far East!

A beat.

It'll be that Oriental over there we'll wonder where the bloody hell we are!

A beat.

DOT She sez she's going down to her Mam's in Nottingham, her next door.

HARRY That'll be good then, the yellow bellied bastards! She'll enjoy it down there! I hope he takes that ladder with him, falls off it, and breaks his bloody neck!

DOT *takes in her home she is very unsettled.*

DOT I've only ever lived here!

A beat.

HARRY I have!

Walls were damp when we first moved in, can tha' remember? the plaster was still drying; and that didn't do my chest any good, I got worse colds working in t' house, than I ever did working at pit.

A beat.

DOT I don't suppose we'll ever come back, will we?

A beat.

HARRY I don't suppose!

A beat.

DOT I'm going miss...

A beat.

I know it's daft but...

DOT *begins to cry.*

It's mi home...

A beat.

HARRY I thought you said there's sod all here?

DOT Oh shut up you! You're not bothered about anybody but yourself!

> **DOT** *is in tears, trying to reconcile herself.* **HARRY** *picks up the cases.*

HARRY Hey this is all about you this...

DOT Aye and if it ends up being shite, it'll be all my fault!

HARRY She had no idea what she was doing, when she closed them pits!

A beat.

DOT She didn't have a bloody clue that woman!

> **HARRY** *picks up the cases.*

HARRY Just like going on t' picket is't it?

A beat.

DOT How is it?

> **HARRY** *screams in aggressive frustration.*

You're bloody barmy!

HARRY Come on you bastards!

> **DOT** *picks up her case.*

DOT You're completely bloody barmy!

HARRY *spots his neighbour.*

HARRY Come on, I'll tek you all on!!

They pick up their cases and move to exit and laugh as they make their way upstage, where they dump the cases as...

Music swells.*

Lights fade.

Black out.

Curtain

---

* A licence to produce *Shafted!* does not include a performance licence for any third-party or copyrighted recordings. Licensees should create their own.

PROPERTY LIST

Props are optional for this play, but in the first production we used:
A garden gate
A bucket
A window cleaner's ladder and cloths
A watering can
A sweeping brush
Beer glasses
A wheelchair
A garden seat
Celebration balloons
Paint and paint brush
A large half painted garden gnome
Two foldable garden seats
A large travel case and a mobile case.

SOUND EFFECTS

In the first production no sound effects were used.

ABOUT THE AUTHOR

John was born the son of a miner in Upton, West Yorkshire. He trained as a teacher in drama at Breton Hall College. Whilst he was Head of Drama at Minsthorpe High School, the school he attended as a student, he won every major award at the National Student Drama Festival between 1981 and 1983.

John has an MA from Leeds University, an Hon DLitt from Hull University, an Hon DLitt from Lincoln University and a DUni from the Open University and was a doctoral research student at Leeds University for five years. He is a Professor of Contemporary Theatre at Liverpool Hope University and a Fellow of the Royal Society of Arts and a Fellow of Regents University, London.

John's plays are performed across the world and he has the distinction of being one of the most performed writers in the English language. He has won numerous awards for his plays including a Laurence Olivier Award and seven Los Angeles Critics' Circle Awards. His plays include *Bouncers, Up 'n' Under, April in Paris, Teechers, Blood Sweat and Tears, Happy Jack, September in the Rain, Salt of the Earth, Passion Killers, Happy Families, Gym & Tonic, Lucky Sods, Unleashed, Thick as a Brick, Men of the World, Perfect Pitch, Muddy Cows* and *Funny Turns*. John also co-wrote the highly successful *Shakers* with Jane Thornton.

John is also co-writer of the BAFTA-award-winning *Oddsquad* and wrote both *Thunder Road* and *My Kingdom for a Horse* (BBC). His first feature film, *Up 'n' Under*, adapted from his own play was released in 1998. For television, John also wrote for *Grange Hill, Brookside* and *Crown Court*.

John has also written extensively for radio, including two series of *Spread a Little Happiness*, which he co-wrote with Jane Thornton for Watershed Productions, *Going East*, also co-written with Jane Thornton and *First Born*, both for the BBC.

John was the Artistic Director of Hull Truck for twenty-five years and helped to design and raise money for the new theatre. He also played a significant role in Hull being named City of Culture 2017.

In 2011, John set up The John Godber Company with Jane Thornton and formed a partnership with Theatre Royal Wakefield to produce two tours of his work each year. To date, plays produced and toured by the JGC include *The Debt Collectors, Weekend Breaks, Teechers, Bouncers, Happy Jack* and *Shafted!*

www.ingramcontent.com/pod-product-compliance
Ingram Content Group UK Ltd.
Pitfield, Milton Keynes, MK11 3LW, UK
UKHW021823150726
7214IPUK00017B/283